Collins

真 学

C000088507

Real Shanghai
Mathematics
Practice Book

3.1

上海教育出版社
SHANGHAI EDUCATIONAL
PUBLISHING HOUSE

世纪出版

MIX
Paper from responsible sources
FSC™ C007454
www.fsc.org

This book is produced from independently certified FSC paper to ensure responsible forest management.
For more information visit: **www.harpercollins.co.uk/green**

William Collins' dream of knowledge for all began with the publication of his first book in 1819. A self-educated mill worker, he not only enriched millions of lives, but also founded a flourishing publishing house. Today, staying true to this spirit, Collins books are packed with inspiration, innovation and practical expertise. They place you at the centre of a world of possibility and give you exactly what you need to explore it.

Collins. Freedom to teach.

Collins
An imprint of HarperCollins*Publishers*
The News Building
1 London Bridge Street
London
SE1 9GF

Browse the complete Collins catalogue at
www.collins.co.uk

Published by arrangement with Shanghai Century Publishing Group Co., Ltd.

10 9 8 7 6 5 4 3

ISBN 978-0-00-826170-2

The educational materials in this book were compiled in accordance with the course curriculum produced by the Shanghai Schools (Pre-Schools) Curriculum Reform Commission and 'Maths Syllabus for Shanghai Schools (Trial Implementation)' for use in Primary 3 First Term under the nine-year compulsory education system.

These educational materials were compiled by the head of Shanghai Normal University, and reviewed and approved for trial use by Shanghai Schools Educational Materials Review Board.

The writers for this book's educational materials are:

Editor-in-Chief: Jianhong Huang
Guest Writers (Listed by Chinese character strokes in surname): Ding Mingjuan, Tong Hui, Song Yongfu, Chen Peiqun, Xu Peijing, Huang Jianhong

This volume's Practice Book was revised by: 'Primary School Maths Practice Book' Compilation Team

British Library Cataloguing in Publication Data
A catalogue record for this publication is available from the British Library.

For the English edition:

Primary Publishing Director: Lee Newman
Primary Publishing Managers: Fiona McGlade, Lizzie Catford
Editorial Project Manager: Mike Appleton
Editorial Manager: Amanda Harman
Editorial Assistant: Holly Blood
Managing Translator: Huang Xingfeng
Translators: Bian Xinyuan, Chen Qingqing, Chen Yilin, Huang Chunhua, Wang Yaqi, Peng Yuyun, Zhu Youqin
Lead Editor: Tanya Solomons
Copyeditor: Joan Miller
Proofreaders: Alison Walters, Helen Bleck, Joan Miller
Cover artist: Amparo Barrera
Designer: Ken Vail Graphic Design
Production Controller: Sarah Burke
Printer: Printed and bound by CPI Group (UK) Ltd, Croydon, CR0 4YY

Photo acknowledgements
The publishers wish to thank the following for permission to reproduce photographs. Every effort has been made to trace copyright holders and to obtain their permission for the use of copyright materials. The publishers will gladly receive any information enabling them to rectify any error or omission at the first opportunity.

(t = top, c = centre, b = bottom, r = right, l = left)

p35 Gino Santa Maria/Shutterstock.com, p35tl Richard Griffin/ Shutterstock.com, p35tr Svitlana-ua/Shutterstock.com, p35c Hong Vo/Shutterstock.com, p35c Alexander Raths/ Shutterstock.com, p38br Alexander Raths/Shutterstock.com, p38l Gino Santa Maria/Shutterstock.com, p38t Paul Wishart/ Shutterstock.com, p38r Richard Griffin/Shutterstock.com, p38b lauraslens/Shutterstock.com, p43l Demja/Shutterstock.com, p43r Bikeworldtravel / Shutterstock.com, p58 Macrovector/ Shutterstock.com, p65 Javen/Shutterstock.com, p71 jemastock/ Fotolia, p72 Shutterstock.com/ Kuryanovich Tatsiana, p81 Shutterstock.com/ Rawpixel.com, p88l Shutterstock.com/ Photology1971, p88r Shutterstock.com/ crystalfoto.

All other images with permission from Shanghai Century Publishing Group.

Contents

Unit One: Revising and improving

Uncle Paulo picked peaches in the orchard. He picked 156 kilograms of peaches on the first day, and he picked 200 kilograms of peaches on the second and third days respectively. How many kilograms of peaches did he pick altogether?

The table below lists the sections in this unit.

After completing each section, assess your work.

(Use 😊 if you are satisfied with your progress or 😐 if you are not satisfied.)

Section	Self-assessment
1. A brief review	
2. Multiply or divide two numbers	
3. Shapes made from squares – polyominoes	

1. A brief review

Pupil Textbook pages 2–5

1. Calculate.

$670 - 250 =$	$340 + 430 =$	$1000 - 600 =$
$185 + 115 =$	$217 - 183 =$	$300 + 700 =$

$9 \times 6 - 4 =$	$10 - 0 \times 9 =$	$12 \div 6 - 2 =$
$12 - 12 \div 3 =$	$6 + 4 \times 3 =$	$48 \div 8 + 8 =$

2. Think and calculate.

$120 + 280 =$	$268 + 132 =$	$546 - 150 =$
$120 + 276 =$	$258 + 142 =$	$556 - 150 =$
$120 + 272 =$	$248 + 152 =$	$566 - 150 =$

3. Work these out, showing the steps in your calculation.

$267 - 152 + 238$	$572 - 138 - 272$	$436 + 187 + 213$

4. Partition and combine.

14 × 7

= (   ) × 7 + (   ) × 7

=

=

4 × 19

=

=

=

---

3 × 5 + 2 × 5

= (   ) × 5

=

=

16 × 5 − 8 × 5

=

=

=

5 Read each question carefully and work out the answer.

a. Uncle Paulo picked peaches in the orchard. He picked 156 kilograms of peaches on the first day, and picked 200 kilograms of peaches on the second and third days respectively. How many kilograms of peaches did he pick?

b. Emma bought two sets of comic books. One set cost £25. The other set was made up of 3 comic books, and each book cost £8. How much did these two sets of comic books cost altogether?

Level **B**

1. Count the shapes.

There are (   ) triangles altogether in this picture.

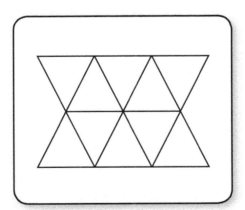

2. There are 25 numbers in the 5 × 5 square in this diagram. Calculate their sum. (   )

1	2	3	4	5
2	3	4	5	1
3	4	5	1	2
4	5	1	2	3
5	1	2	3	4

2. Multiply or divide two numbers

Pupil Textbook pages 6–7

Level **A**

1. Calculate.

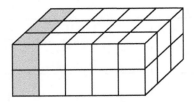

There are (   ) blocks in the coloured column, and there are (   ) columns, so there are (   ) blocks in total.

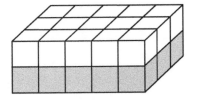

There are (   ) blocks in the coloured row, and there are (   ) rows, so there are (   ) blocks in total.

2. Work these out, showing the steps in your calculation.

a. Multiply by two numbers.

$4 \times 3 \times 2$

$0 \times 10 \times 6$

$3 \times 2 \times 8$

b. Divide by two numbers.

$18 \div 2 \div 3$

$45 \div 5 \div 3$

$64 \div 8 \div 2$

3. Multiple choice – write the letter of the correct answer in the brackets.

a. How many metres has the swimmer swum? The correct number sentence is (   ).

He has swum 3 lengths in the 25-metre lane.

A. 25 × 3   **B.** 25 × 2   **C.** 25 × 2 × 3   **D.** 25 × 3 × 2 × 2

b. The teacher bought prizes for hard-working pupils. He spent £120 on 3 boxes of pens. Each box has 8 pens. How much does each pen cost? The correct number sentence is (   ).
   A. 120 ÷ 3 × 8   **B.** 120 ÷ 8 × 3   **C.** 120 ÷ 3 ÷ 8   **D.** 120 × 3 × 8

c. Year 3 pupils donated money to a homeless charity. The average donation was £5 each. There are 40 pupils in each class. There are 4 classes in the whole of Year 3. How much was the total donation? The correct number sentence is (   ).
   A. 40 × 5 ÷ 4   **B.** 40 × 5 × 4   **C.** 40 ÷ 5 × 4   **D.** 40 ÷ 5 ÷ 4

4. Read each question carefully and work out the answer.

The pupils were preparing a party to celebrate Easter.

a. The pupils made 81 paper Easter eggs. They tied 9 paper Easter eggs together to make a string and gave 3 strings of paper Easter eggs to each group in the party. How many groups can receive these strings of Easter eggs?

b. The teacher bought some fruit for the pupils in Year 3. There are 5 classes in Year 3. Each class has 4 groups, and each group was given 2 kilograms of fruit. How many kilograms of fruit did the teacher buy altogether?

1. To prepare the school for parents' evening the corridor was decorated with pupils' paintings. There are 8 classes in Year 1 and Year 2. Each class gave 5 paintings. In total, the number of paintings from Year 3, Year 4 and Year 5 was 2 times the number of paintings from Year 1 and Year 2. How many paintings by pupils in Year 3, Year 4 and Year 5 were used altogether?

2. Pupils held a talent competition in the school hall. There were 16 entries in total. Half of the entries won prizes for effort and half of the remainder won prizes for attitude. How many entries won prizes for attitude?

3. Shapes made from squares – polyominoes

Level **A**

1. Sort these shapes by counting the squares in each one.

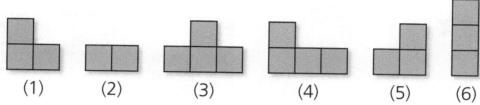

(1)   (2)   (3)   (4)   (5)   (6)

2-polyominoes: _____   3-polyominoes: _____

4-polyominoes: _____

2. Multiple choice – write the letter of the correct answer in the brackets.

a.

We can cut out (   ) at most from the 4 × 4 square

A. 3   **B.** 4   **C.** 5   **D.** 6

b. The only 4-polyomino that cannot be formed by adding 1 square to 3-polyomino 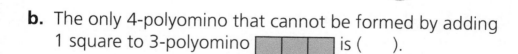 is (   ).

A.   **B.**   **C.**   **D.**

1. Form a 4 × 3 rectangle with these polyominoes.
(Shade the rectangle with different colours to represent
the polyominoes.)

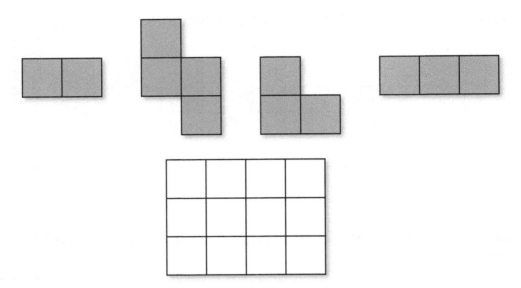

2. Partition the numeral 9 diagrams with different 4-polyomino
shapes. Colour them on the diagram.

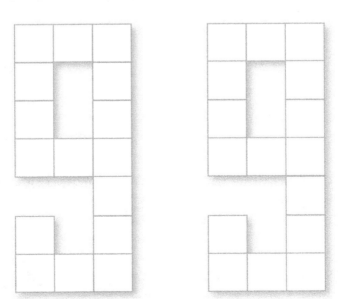

Unit Two: Multiplying by a one-digit number

The spaceship takes 90 minutes to orbit Earth, circling it once. Can it make 3 orbits of Earth in 4 hours?

The table below lists the sections in this unit.

After completing each section, assess your work.

(Use 😊 if you are satisfied with your progress or 😐 if you are not satisfied.)

Section	
1. Multiplying by multiples of 10 and 100	
2. Writing number sentences	
3. Multiplying a two-digit number by a one-digit number	
4. Multiplying a three-digit number by a one-digit number	
5. Practice exercise (1)	

1. Multiplying by multiples of 10 and 100

Pupil Textbook pages 10–13   Level **A**

1. Work these out. Think about your work.

2 × 3 =	6 × 7 =	9 × 8 =
2 × 30 =	6 × 70 =	9 × 80 =
2 × 300 =	6 × 700 =	9 × 800 =
20 × 3 =	60 × 7 =	90 × 8 =

2. Calculate.

20 × 5 + 10 =	3 × 800 – 20 =	2 × 2 × 30 =
500 – 7 × 70 =	60 + 90 × 6 =	300 × 3 × 6 =

3. Write >, < or = in the ◯ to make the number sentences true.

9 × 50 ◯ 90 × 5   40 × 6 ◯ 3 × 70   8 × 200 ◯ 500 × 6

4. Read each question carefully and work out the answer.

a. There are 5 packs of printing paper in each box
and there are 500 sheets of printing paper in each pack.
How many sheets of printing paper are there in each box?

b. There are 300 car parking spaces in a housing estate in Shanghai. The number of parking spaces for bicycles is 9 times the number for cars. How many parking spaces for bicycles are there altogether in this estate?

c. A moped workshop wants to assemble 200 electric mopeds. They have 420 wheels. Is this enough?

Level **B**

The spaceship takes 90 minutes to orbit Earth, circling it once. Can it make 3 orbits of Earth in 4 hours?

2. Writing number sentences

Pupil Textbook pages 14–15

1. Calculate.

60 × 7 =

400 × 5 =

3 × 400 =

40 × 5 × 6 =

8 × 50 =

20 × 5 × 9 =

2. Draw lines to match the conditions and the questions they relate to. Then write the correct number sentences – but do not calculate the answers.

There are 4 bags of biscuits in each packet.	1. Emma's family bought 3 boxes of peaches. How much did they cost?
There are 36 peaches in each box.	2. How much do 5 packets of rice cost?
Each box of peaches costs £58.	3. How many bags of biscuits are there in 25 packets?
Each packet of rice costs £88.	4. Dylan's family bought 4 boxes of peaches. How many peaches are there altogether?

Write number sentences.

a. _____   b. _____

c. _____   d. _____

3. Read each question carefully and work out the answer.

a. There are 4 bags of biscuits in each packet.
How many bags of biscuits are there in 20 packets altogether?

b. Poppy's family bought 5 boxes of kiwi fruits. There are 30 kiwi fruits in each box and each box. How many kiwi fruits did they buy in all?

c. A shopkeeper sold £4000 worth of stock each month in half a year and purchased £9000 worth of stock in this time. How much profit did she make?

The supermarket is having a sales promotion.

The promotion offer states:
Spend over £300 for a discount of £20.
Spend over £500 for a discount of £50.

a. For a school disco, Alex's mother bought 50 boxes of chocolate biscuits. Each box costs £6. Think about it – how much should Alex's mother actually pay?

b. Alex's father bought 70 crates of milk. Each box costs £9. How much discount can his father get, at most? How much should Alex's father actually pay?

3. Multiplying a two-digit number by a one-digit number

Pupil Textbook page 16

1. Calculate.

$42 \times 2 = \boxed{84}$

$40 \times 2 = \boxed{80}$

$2 \times 2 = \boxed{4}$

$80 + 4 = \boxed{84}$

$99 \times 6 = \boxed{}$

$90 \times 6 = \boxed{}$

$9 \times 6 = \boxed{}$

$\boxed{} + \boxed{} = \boxed{}$

$7 \times 35 = \boxed{}$

$7 \times 30 = \boxed{}$

$7 \times 5 = \boxed{}$

$\boxed{} + \boxed{} = \boxed{}$

2. Work these out, showing the steps in your calculation.

$6 \times 53 =$

$31 \times 4 =$

$8 \times 47 =$

---

3. Read each question carefully and work out the answer.

a. The Model Club takes 35 minutes to make a model ship. How long will it take to make 5 model ships?

b. Each box of yogurt costs the supermarket £7.05. How much do 6 boxes of yogurt cost?

Level **B**

1. There are 9 rows of apple trees and 9 rows of plum trees in the orchard. There are 36 trees in each row. How many trees are there in the orchard altogether?

2. 59×7

$= 50 \times 7 + 9 \times 7$

$= 350 + 63$

$= 413$

Can you calculate 59 × 7 in another way? Try it out.

Pupil Textbook page 17

Level **A**

1. Fill in the missing numbers.

$$
\begin{array}{r}
5\ 2 \\
\times\qquad 4 \\
\hline
8 \\
2\ 0\ 0 \\
\hline
2\ 0\ 8
\end{array}
$$

··· (   ) × (   )

··· (   ) × (   )

2. Use the column method to solve the number problems.

$32 \times 3 =$ $41 \times 6 =$ $4 \times 52 =$

3. Fill in the missing numbers.

a. When you calculate 62×4, the product of the 6 in the tens place times 4 is (   ).

b. When you calculate 8☐ × 4, the product in the ones place is 8. Therefore, the digit in the ☐ may be (   ).

c. The product of ☐3 × 3 is a three-digit number. The smallest number that can be written in the ☐ is (   ).

d. When you multiply a two-digit number by a one-digit number, the product may be a (   )-digit number or a (   )-digit number.

4. Read the question carefully and work out the answer.

A leopard has a mass of 72 kilograms, and the mass of a tiger is 4 times that of a leopard. What is the mass of the tiger?

1. The picture shows 4 boxes of biscuits.

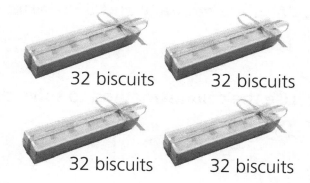

32 biscuits   32 biscuits

32 biscuits   32 biscuits

 a. How many biscuits are there altogether?

 b. Are there enough biscuits to share among 21 pupils so that each pupil will get 5 biscuits?

2. To organise a party for a local nursing home, Dylan, Alex, Poppy and Emma raised money by doing a sponsored shoe-shine. They used the money to buy some special food and pay a singer to entertain the residents. This table shows the money that the pupils brought to school.

Denomination (£)	50	20	10	5	1
Number of notes or coins	1	5	2	6	18

They bought 3 boxes of cakes and paid for the singer with this money. We know that each box of cakes costs £23. How much does the singer cost?

Pupil Textbook page 18

1. Calculate mentally and then write the answers.

12 × 3 =   21 × 5 =   6 × 41 =

2. Use the column method to solve the number problems.

15 × 3 =   38 × 2 =   4 × 17 =

3. Read each question carefully and work out the answer.

a. The clocks show the times when Dylan leaves home and arrives at school. Father's journey to work takes 4 times as long as Dylan's journey to school. How long does Dylan's father take to get to work?

Leave home

Arrive at school

b. These are the prices of goods sold in a shop.

Picture	Notebook	Card
£8	£4	£2

i. How much do 24 cards cost?

ii. How much do 1 picture and 32 notebooks cost altogether?

iii. If you had £130 could you buy 33 notebooks?

30 pupils from each of Class 1 and Class 2 in Year 3 take part in a basketball competition. All the pupils in Class 1 and 29 pupils in Class 2 took their turn at scoring a basket. Each of these pupils scored 3 baskets. If the last pupil in Class 2 scores 4 baskets, the total points for Class 2 will be higher than the total for Class 1. How many baskets have been scored by each class? What is the difference in scores between Class 1 and Class 2?

Pupil Textbook page 19

1. First, write two numbers between which you estimate the product to be. Then use the column method to work out the answer.

$5 \times 78 =$

My estimate:

$5 \times 70 =$

$5 \times 80 =$

The product is between (   ) and (   ).

By the column method:

$82 \times 6 =$

My estimate:

(   ) $\times 6 =$

(   ) $\times 6 =$

The product is between (   ) and (   ).

By the column method:

2. Are the following calculations correct? Put a tick (✓) for 'correct' or a cross (✗) for 'incorrect' in the brackets. Then show the correct calculation for any that are wrong.

```
      1 3              6 1              1 6
  ×     6          ×     5          ×     6
  ─────────        ─────────        ─────────
      6 8          3 0 5            6 3 6
  (      )          (      )          (      )
```

The correct calculation:

3. Use the column method to complete the number sentences.

3 × 56 =   28 × 7 =   75 × 8 =

4. Read each question carefully and work out the answer.

   a. There are 4 rows of flowers by the path from the school gate to the main door of the school and there are 38 pots in each row. How many pots of flowers are there in 4 rows?

   b. A crane has a mass of 9 kilograms and an ostrich has a mass 13 times that of the crane. What is the mass of the ostrich?

   c. Alex reads a comic book. He reads 16 pages every day. There are 7 pages left after he has been reading for 8 days. How many pages has Alex read in 8 days? How many pages are there in this comic book in total?

1. The pupils in Year 3 go on an autumn school trip. Each bus can carry 45 people. 4 of the buses are full but there are 17 empty seats on the fifth bus. How many people altogether went on the school trip?

2. Write the missing numbers in the boxes.

$$
\begin{array}{r}
5\ \square \\
\times\quad 6 \\
\hline
\square\ 3\ 6
\end{array}
\qquad
\begin{array}{r}
\square\ 8 \\
\times\quad 7 \\
\hline
\square\ 0\ 6
\end{array}
$$

4. Multiplying a three-digit number by a one-digit number

Pupil Textbook page 20

1. Calculate.

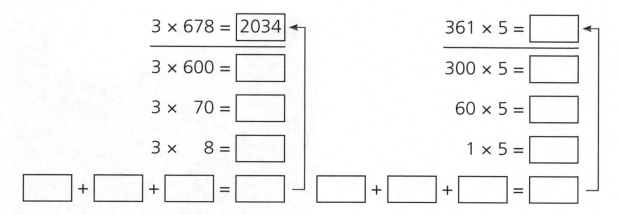

$$3 \times 678 = \boxed{2034}$$
$$3 \times 600 = \boxed{}$$
$$3 \times 70 = \boxed{}$$
$$3 \times 8 = \boxed{}$$
$$\boxed{} + \boxed{} + \boxed{} = \boxed{}$$

$$361 \times 5 = \boxed{}$$
$$300 \times 5 = \boxed{}$$
$$60 \times 5 = \boxed{}$$
$$1 \times 5 = \boxed{}$$
$$\boxed{} + \boxed{} + \boxed{} = \boxed{}$$

2. Write the calculation in full, showing your working.

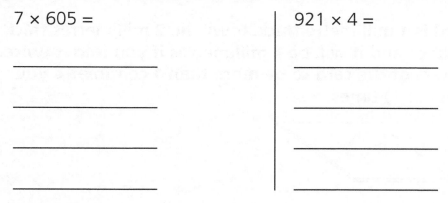

$7 \times 605 =$

_____

_____

_____

_____

$921 \times 4 =$

_____

_____

_____

_____

3. True or false? Put a tick (✓) for 'true' or a cross (✗) for 'false' in the brackets.

a. $912 \times 4 = 9 \times 4 + 1 \times 4 + 2 \times 4$ (   )

b. $5 \times 102 = 100 \times 5 + 2 \times 5$ (   )

4. Read the question carefully and work out the answer.

Dylan went on a trip to a museum in Paris with his parents. Each ticket costs £185. How much did they spend altogether?

A piece of card is 1 millimetre thick. It will be 2 millimetres thick if you fold it once and it will be 4 millimetres if you fold it twice. For the thickness of the card to be more than 1 centimetre you have to fold it (   ) times.

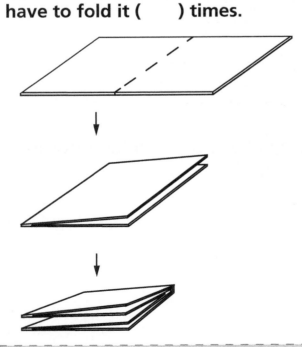

1. Write the missing numbers in the brackets.

$$
\begin{array}{r}
4\ 5\ 7 \\
\times \quad\quad 3 \\
\hline
2\ 1 \\
1\ 5\ 0 \\
1\ 2\ 0\ 0 \\
\hline
1\ 3\ 7\ 1 \\
\end{array}
$$

$\cdots\ (\qquad) \times (\qquad)$
$\cdots\ (\qquad) \times (\qquad)$
$\cdots\ (\qquad) \times (\qquad)$
$\cdots\ (\qquad) + (\qquad) + (\qquad)$

2. Use the column method to calculate then write the correct letters in the spaces in the sentence below.

A. $212 \times 4 =$ **B.** $113 \times 8 =$

C. $5 \times 321 =$ **D.** $264 \times 4 =$

The product of _____ are three-digit numbers; the product of _____ are four-digit numbers.

3. Are the following calculations correct? Put a tick (✓) for 'correct' or a cross (✗) for 'incorrect' in the brackets. Then show the correct calculation for any that are wrong.

$$
\begin{array}{r}
2\ 7\ 6 \\
\times \quad\quad 4 \\
\hline
8\ 0\ 4 \\
\end{array}
\qquad
\begin{array}{r}
8\ 3\ 2 \\
\times \quad\quad 5 \\
\hline
4\ 1\ 5\ 0 \\
\end{array}
\qquad
\begin{array}{r}
6\ 0\ 3 \\
\times \quad\quad 7 \\
\hline
4\ 2\ 2\ 1 \\
\end{array}
$$

(   )   (   )   (   )

The correct calculation:

4. Use the column method to complete the number sentences.

301 × 2 =   409 × 3 =   204 × 5 =

5. Multiple choice – write the letter of the correct answer in the brackets.

a. The product of 6 × 705 has (   ) 0s.

A. 1   **B.** 2   **C.** 3

b. 193 × 2 + 193 (   ) 193 × 3

A. <   **B.** =   **C.** >

c. Look at these number sentences. Without calculating, the one with the greatest product is (   ).

A. 809 × 4   **B.** 809 × 5   **C.** 908 × 5

6. Read each question carefully and work out the answer.

a. The height of a deer is 128 centimetres.
The height of a giraffe is 4 times that of a deer.
How tall is a giraffe?

b. There are 118 seats in one train carriage. How many seats are there in 8 train carriages?

c. A school took part in a local conservation activity. The Year 3 pupils and teachers collected 305 batteries in all. The number of batteries collected by Year 5 pupils and teachers is 3 times the number collected by Year 3 pupils and teachers. How many batteries did the pupils and teachers of Year 5 collect?

d. One morning, 3 parties of pupils visited a museum, with 207 pupils in each party. 469 pupils visited the museum in the afternoon. How many pupils visited the museum in the morning? How many pupils visited the museum on this day?

Level **B**

Think and calculate.

$2 \times 99 =$ $2 \times 999 =$

$3 \times 99 =$ $3 \times 999 =$

$4 \times 99 =$ $4 \times 999 =$

$5 \times 99 =$ $5 \times 999 =$

$6 \times 99 =$ $6 \times 999 =$

$7 \times 99 =$ $7 \times 999 =$

$8 \times 99 =$ $8 \times 999 =$

Tell me what you have found.

Pupil Textbook page 22

1. Use the column method to complete the number sentences.

610 × 3 =   450 × 6 =   8 × 320 =

2. Fill in the missing numbers.

a. The product of 850 × 4 has (   ) 0s. The middle two digits in the product of 301 × 7 have (   ) 0s.

b. Poppy's first number is 960 and her second number is 3 times her first number, so her second number is (   ). Her third number is 906 less than the second number, so her third number is (   ). Now write the three numbers in order, from smallest to largest. (   )

c. 205 $\xrightarrow{\times 2}$ (   ) $\xrightarrow{\times 5}$ (   ) $\xrightarrow{-1095}$ (   ) $\xrightarrow{\times 4}$ (   )

d. If the product of 2☐ × 5 ends with one 0, the number in the ☐ is (   ); if the product of 2☐ × 5 ends with two 0s, the number in the ☐ is (   ).

3. Read each question carefully and work out the answer.

a. In the men's relay race at the sportsground, each person runs 400 metres. How far do 4 men run in the relay, altogether?

b. Charlie's rope is 250 centimetres long. Dylan has a longer rope. It is 4 times the length of Charlie's rope. How long is Dylan's rope?

c. The gardeners planted 170 pines in the botanical gardens. Then they planted 3 times as many Chinese parasol trees as pines.

i. How many Chinese parasol trees did they plant altogether?

ii. How many Chinese parasol trees and pines did they plant in all?

Practice: Try it out first, and then fill in the brackets.

Run (   ) metres in 1 minute.
Run about (   ) metres in 2 minutes.

Pulse beats (   ) times in 1 minute.
Pulse beats about (   ) times in 7 minutes.

Write (   ) words in 1 minute.
Write about (   ) words in 10 minutes.

Skip (   ) times in 1 minute.
Skip about (   ) times in 5 minutes.

5. Practice exercise (1)

1. Calculate.

4 × 12 =	900 × 8 =	5 × 60 =
4 × 120 =	9 × 80 =	500 × 6 =

2. Which number sentences have products greater than 3000? Circle them.

8 × 401   905 × 3   690 × 5   4 × 702

3. Use the column method to complete these number sentences.

273 × 4 =   5 × 308 =   690 × 6 =

4. Work these out, showing the steps in your calculation.

230 × 4 + 300   1570 – 5 × 314

109 × 9 – 4 × 109   750 × 8 + 750 × 2

5. Write >, < or = in each ◯ to make the number sentence correct.

102 × 3 ◯ 500   25 × 4 ◯ 5 × 24

43 × 3 ◯ 43 × 7   16 × 2 + 16 × 3 + 16 × 4 ◯ 9 × 16

6. True or false? Put a tick (✓) for 'true' or a cross (✗) for 'false' in the brackets.

a. In the calculation 79 × 6, the number in the tens place of the first factor, 7, times the second factor, 6, is 42.   (   )

b. 0 + 1 + 2 + ⋯ + 10 < 0 × 1 × 2 ⋯ × 10   (   )

7. Read each question carefully and work out the answer.

a. The length of a grasshopper is 8 centimetres and it can jump 16 times its body length. How far can this grasshopper jump?

b. Poppy can type 42 words in 1 minute.

i. How many words can Poppy type in 5 minutes at this rate?

ii. Poppy types an article with 508 words. After 5 minutes, how many words are left for her to type?

iii. If she has 8 minutes more, can she finish this article?

8. Look at the price list below.

A pair of trainers	A computer console	A bicycle
£56	£230	£128

a. How much do 2 bicycles and 1 pair of trainers cost in total?

b. Think of some more maths questions using this information. Write a maths question on the line and then answer it.

My question: _____

The number sentence: _____

The answer: _____

 Level **B**

The products of 502 × 4, 250 × 6 and 525 × 2 are, respectively, the last 4 digits of the number plates of the 3 cars below. Calculate the last 4 numbers of the number plates and write them in the spaces below the 3 cars.

This one has one 0 at the end and one 0 in the middle.

There are two 0s in the middle.

This one ends in two 0s.

Unit Three: Introduction to time (3)

Look at these foods. What are the occasions when you would eat them?

The table below lists the sections in this unit.

After completing each section, assess your work.

(Use 😊 if you are satisfied with your progress or 🙁 if you are not satisfied.)

Section	Self-assessment
1. Years, months and days	
2. Standard years and leap years	
3. Make a calendar	
4. Practice exercise (2)	

1. Years, months and days

Pupil Textbook pages 26–28

Level **A**

1. Look at the 2017 calendar and fill in the missing numbers below.

2017

January
S	M	T	W	T	F	S
1	2	3	4	5	6	7
8	9	10	11	12	13	14
15	16	17	18	19	20	21
22	23	24	25	26	27	28
29	30	31				

February
S	M	T	W	T	F	S
			1	2	3	4
5	6	7	8	9	10	11
12	13	14	15	16	17	18
19	20	21	22	23	24	25
26	27	28				

March
S	M	T	W	T	F	S
			1	2	3	4
5	6	7	8	9	10	11
12	13	14	15	16	17	18
19	20	21	22	23	24	25
26	27	28	29	30	31	

April
S	M	T	W	T	F	S
						1
2	3	4	5	6	7	8
9	10	11	12	13	14	15
16	17	18	19	20	21	22
23	24	25	26	27	28	29
30						

May
S	M	T	W	T	F	S
	1	2	3	4	5	6
7	8	9	10	11	12	13
14	15	16	17	18	19	20
21	22	23	24	25	26	27
28	29	30	31			

June
S	M	T	W	T	F	S
				1	2	3
4	5	6	7	8	9	10
11	12	13	14	15	16	17
18	19	20	21	22	23	24
25	26	27	28	29	30	

July
S	M	T	W	T	F	S
						1
2	3	4	5	6	7	8
9	10	11	12	13	14	15
16	17	18	19	20	21	22
23	24	25	26	27	28	29
30	31					

August
S	M	T	W	T	F	S
		1	2	3	4	5
6	7	8	9	10	11	12
13	14	15	16	17	18	19
20	21	22	23	24	25	26
27	28	29	30	31		

September
S	M	T	W	T	F	S
					1	2
3	4	5	6	7	8	9
10	11	12	13	14	15	16
17	18	19	20	21	22	23
24	25	26	27	28	29	30

October
S	M	T	W	T	F	S
1	2	3	4	5	6	7
8	9	10	11	12	13	14
15	16	17	18	19	20	21
22	23	24	25	26	27	28
29	30	31				

November
S	M	T	W	T	F	S
			1	2	3	4
5	6	7	8	9	10	11
12	13	14	15	16	17	18
19	20	21	22	23	24	25
26	27	28	29	30		

December
S	M	T	W	T	F	S
					1	2
3	4	5	6	7	8	9
10	11	12	13	14	15	16
17	18	19	20	21	22	23
24	25	26	27	28	29	30
31						

a. i. There are _____ months in a year.

ii. _____ have 31 days.

iii. _____ have 30 days.

iv. February had _____ days in 2017.

b. Write the day for each date.

1 / 1 / 2017 _____   3 / 8 / 2017 _____

5 / 1 / 2017 _____   10 / 1 / 2017 _____

2. In 2017, what were the dates of the holidays in the table? What days of the week did they fall on?

	New Year's Day	May Day Bank Holiday	Christmas Day	August Bank Holiday
Dates in numbers				
Days of the week				

3. The abbreviated date 03.12.2020 can be expressed as 3 December, 2020.

Write these abbreviated dates as day, month, year.

a. 13.04.2010
(   )

b. 08.08.2008
(   )

c. 30.05.2009
(   )

4. Write these dates in abbreviated form.

a. 1 June, 2004
(   )

b. 4 May, 1991
(   )

c. 1 May, 2010
(   )

5. Choose the most appropriate answer.

a. There are (   ) days from 20 May to the last day of May.
    A. 9   **B.** 10   **C.** 11   **D.** 12

b. There were (   ) days in the first quarter of 2018.
    A. 88   **B.** 89   **C.** 90   **D.** 91

c. The second day after 29 September, 2009 is (   ).
    A. 27./09   **B.** 31./09   **C.** 01./10   **D.** 02./10

6. True or false? Put a tick (✓) for 'true' or a cross (✗) for 'false' in the brackets.

    a. The odd-numbered months always have 31 days.   (   )

    b. There are 182 days in the first half of each year.   (   )

    c. In November, when 17 days have passed there are
        13 days left.   (   )

    d. The months of February, April, June, September,
        November all have 30 days.   (   )

    e. 4 September, 2013 is a Wednesday, so the 11th, 18th
        and 25th of this month are all Wednesdays.   (   )

Level B

1. On which days do Christmas Day, New Year's Eve, May Day, Spring Bank Holiday and August Bank Holiday occur this year?

2. Make a calendar for February of this year.

Sunday	Monday	Tuesday	Wednesday	Thursday	Friday	Saturday

2. Standard years and leap years

Level **A**

1. This table lists the number of days in February from 2007 to 2020. In these years, which years were standard years? Which years were leap years? What do you notice?

Year	2007	2008	2009	2010	2011	2012	2013
Number of days in February	28	29	28	28	28	29	28
Year	2014	2015	2016	2017	2018	2019	2020
Number of days in February	28	28	29	28	28	28	29

The years from 2007 to 2020:

Standard years: _____

Leap years: _____

You find that: _____

2. Fill in the missing numbers.

a. 2011 is a standard year, the next leap year is (   ) year(s) later, and the previous leap year was (   ) .

b. 1892 was a leap year, so the next leap year was (   ).

c. The leap years from 1990 to 2010 were (   ).

d. Which of these years were leap years? Tick (✔) the brackets under the leap year numbers.

1994	1960	1984	2003	2000	1900
( )	( )	( )	( )	( )	( )

Level **B**

Multiple choice – write the letter of the correct answer in the brackets.

a. There are (   ) days in the first quarter of a leap year.

   A. 89   **B.** 90   **C.** 91   **D.** Uncertain

b. In 2015, Charlie was 11 years old. His birthday is 29 February. He has had (   ) birthdays. (Omit his birth year.)

   A. 11   **B.** 2   **C.** 3   **D.** 4

3. Make a calendar

Pupil Textbook page 31

Complete the calendar for December this year, then use it to make a calendar for next year. (You can choose how to decorate your calendar.)

(   )

Sunday	Monday	Tuesday	Wednesday	Thursday	Friday	Saturday

(   )   (   )   (   )

S	M	T	W	T	F	S

S	M	T	W	T	F	S

S	M	T	W	T	F	S

(   )   (   )   (   )

S	M	T	W	T	F	S

S	M	T	W	T	F	S

S	M	T	W	T	F	S

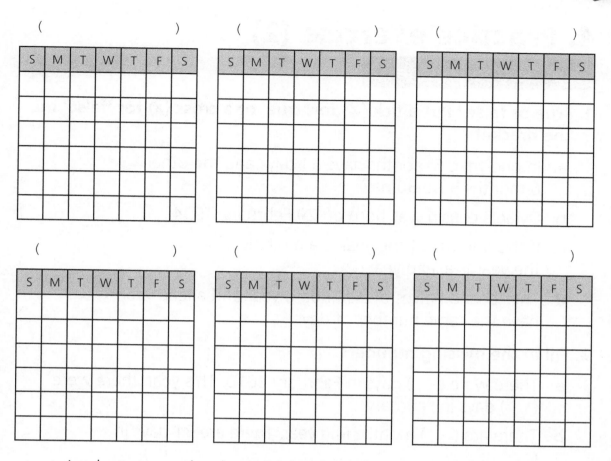

(   )   (   )   (   )

S	M	T	W	T	F	S

a. Look at your calendar. Which month has the most Sundays?

b. What are the dates of your family's birthdays? Use coloured pencils to mark them on the calendar. Don't forget to send your best wishes to them.

c. What other important days do you know? Find out their dates and write them in your calendar.

4. Practice exercise (2)

Pupil Textbook page 32
Level **A**

1. True or false? Put a tick (✓) for 'true' or a cross (✗) for 'false' in the brackets.

    a. In one year, 6 months have 31 days and the other 6 months have 30 days. ( )

    b. Dylan's cousin was born on 29 February, 1994. ( )

    c. If the number of the year is a multiple of 4, the year is a leap year. ( )

    d. The second halves of a standard year and a leap year have the same number of days. ( )

2. Fill in the missing numbers.

    a. There were ( ) days in February 2010. This year, there were ( ) days in February.

    b. There are ( ) months in a year. There are 31 days in
( ).
There are 30 days in ( ).
There are ( ) days in February in a standard year. There are ( ) days in February in a leap year.

    c. 2016 was a ( ) year, the next leap year is ( ).

    d. 4 years and 7 months = ( ) months

Level **B**

Jacob stayed at his grandmother's house for a period of 62 days, and this was exactly two months. So these two months were ( ) and ( ) or ( ) and ( ).

Mia stayed at her grandmother's house for two months. She stayed for at least ( ) days.

Unit Four: Dividing by a one-digit number

Can you divide the drums in the array into 4 groups?

The table below lists the sections in this unit.

After completing each section, assess your work.

(Use 😊 if you are satisfied with your progress or 😐 if you are not satisfied.)

Section	
1. Dividing a multiple of 10 or a multiple of 100	
2. Dividing a two-digit number by a one-digit number	
3. Dividing a three-digit number by a one-digit number	
4. Applications of division	
5. Unit price, quantity and total price	
6. Practice exercise (3)	

1. Dividing a multiple of 10 or a multiple of 100

Pupil Textbook page 34

Level **A**

1. Calculate.

$720 \div 9 =$	$700 \div 7 =$	$560 \div 8 =$
$200 \div 5 =$	$100 \div 5 =$	$400 \div 8 =$

2. Read each question carefully and work out the answer.

The book has 270 pages. I have read 90 pages.

a. i. How many pages does the boy have left to read?

   ii. He needs to read the rest of the pages in 3 days.
       How many pages must he read each day?

b. Ravi is set 120 mental calculations to do in 3 weeks.
   How many calculations must Ravi do each week?

Level **B**

**Look at the diagram carefully.
What numbers could you write in
the brackets?**

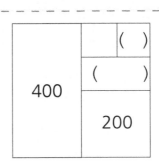

2. Dividing a two-digit number by a one-digit number

Pupil Textbook page 35

Level **A**

1. Calculate.

84 ÷ 7 =
70 ÷ 7 =
14 ÷ 7 =

89 ÷ 6 =
60 ÷ 6 =
29 ÷ 6 =

87 ÷ 7 =

----

96 ÷ 8 =
80 ÷ 8 =
----

91 ÷ 6 =
60 ÷ 6 =
----

79 ÷ 5 =

----

2. Read each question carefully and work out the answer.

   a. A restaurant has 73 kilograms of potatoes and 6 kilograms of tomatoes. The mass of the potatoes is how many times the mass of the tomatoes?

   b. Emma plans to finish 96 calculations in 8 days. How many calculations does she need to do each day?

   c. There are 52 tennis balls. If 3 tennis balls are put in each small bucket, how many buckets can be filled at most? How many tennis balls will be left over?

Which fruit is cheaper?

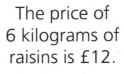

The price of
6 kilograms of
raisins is £12.

The price of
4 kilograms of
strawberries is £14.

1. Column method

$75 \div 3 =$ | $91 \div 2 =$ | $81 \div 5 =$ | $70 \div 5 =$ | $47 \div 6 =$

2. Fill in the missing numbers.

```
      2 9
  3 ) 8 7
      6          3 × (   ) = (   )
    ─────
      2 7
      2 7        3 × (   ) = (   )
    ─────
        0
```

```
      2 3
  4 ) 9 5
      8          (   ) × (   ) = (   )
    ─────
      1 5
      1 2        (   ) × (   ) = (   )
    ─────
        3
```

3. Are the following calculations correct? Put a tick (✓) for 'correct' or a cross (✗) for 'incorrect' in the brackets. Then show the correct calculation for any that are wrong.

```
      1 4
  4 ) 6 3
      4
    ─────
      2 3
      1 6
    ─────
        7
    (     )
```

```
      4 7
  2 ) 9 5
      8
    ─────
      1 5
      1 4
    ─────
        1
    (     )
```

```
        5
  8 ) 4 6
      4 0
    ─────
        6
    (     )
```

The correct calculation:

4. Read each question carefully and work out the answer.

a. The school model-making club has 60 members.
The members are divided into groups of 4.
How many groups will there be?

b. Dylan took 78 photos during the summer holidays. He prints
them out and puts them into a photo album that holds 4 photos
on each page. How many pages can he fill completely? How
many photos will be left over?

c. A bag contains 52 sweets. If the sweets are shared equally
among 3 people, how many sweets will each person get?

d. There are 89 pictures of the 2010 Shanghai world expo mascot
'China'. Calculate and fill in the blanks.

Divided equally among 3 groups	Each group gets ( ) pictures.	( ) pictures are left.
Divided equally among 5 groups	Each group gets ( ) pictures.	( ) pictures are left.
Divided equally among 7 groups	Each group gets ( ) pictures.	( ) pictures are left.
Divided equally among 9 groups	Each group gets ( ) pictures.	( ) pictures are left.

I eat about 42 insects in 3 days.

Jeremy

I eat about 91 insects in a week.

Emily

What maths questions about these frogs can you think of? Write your questions, then write number sentences and solve them.

a. Question: _____

   Number sentence: _____

   Answer: _____

b. Question: _____

   Number sentence: _____

   Answer: _____

4 Dividing by a one-digit number

 Level **A**

1. Calculate.

63 ÷ 3 = | 96 ÷ 8 = | 88 ÷ 4 = | 90 ÷ 3 =

2. Look at the number sentences. Then write the letters of the correct calculations in the brackets.

A. 91 ÷ 7 = | **B.** 78 ÷ 8 = | **C.** 57 ÷ 2 =

D. 56 ÷ 6 = | **E.** 89 ÷ 4 = | **F.** 83 ÷ 4 =

The quotient is a one-digit number in (   ).

The quotient is a two-digit number in (   ).

3. Use the column method to calculate and then check your answers.

80 ÷ 6 = | 91 ÷ 3 =

4. Three groups of pupils in Year 3 at Faraday Primary School were collecting used batteries.

	First group	Second group	Third group
Number of pupils	4	5	3
Number of used batteries	56	75	39
Average number of batteries collected by each pupil			

Which group of pupils collected the most batteries? (   )

5. Read each question carefully and work out the answer.

   a. Divide 75 stickers equally among 7 children. How many stickers will each child get? How many stickers are left over?

   b. 82 stickers were divided equally among 7 children and 5 stickers were left over. How many stickers did each child get?

1. Fill in the missing numbers.

   a. Write a suitable number in each ☐.

   ☐☐ $\div 5 = 18$ r 1

   b. What is the greatest number you can write in the ◯ to make the number sentence correct?

   ◯ $\div 6 = 6$ r ☐

2. 40 ÷ ☐ **=** ☐ **r 4**

   The divisor is a one-digit number, which could be ( ).

3. Dividing a three-digit number by a one-digit number

Pupil Textbook pages 40–41

Level **A**

1. **What is the greatest number that can go in the brackets?**

(   ) × 4 < 35   7 × (   ) < 48   (   ) × 8 < 63

2. Calculate.

672 ÷ 6 =	481 ÷ 2 =	218 ÷ 4 =
600 ÷ 6 =	400 ÷ 2 =	200 ÷ 4 =
60 ÷ 6 =	80 ÷ 2 =	18 ÷ 4 =
12 ÷ 6 =	1 ÷ 2 =	

893 ÷ 4 =   723 ÷ 8 =   785 ÷ 3 =

3. **Estimate the number of digits that the quotient will have. Then calculate, using the column method.**

Check the number sentences marked with * and show the steps in your calculation.

788 ÷ 3 =   705 ÷ 5 =   890 ÷ 8 =

Estimate: Estimate: Estimate:
Quotient is a   Quotient is a   Quotient is a
( )-digit number   ( )-digit number   ( )-digit number

*940 ÷ 3 =   *821 ÷ 7 =

Estimate: Estimate:
Quotient is a   Quotient is a
( )-digit number   ( )-digit number

4. Read each question carefully and work out the answer.

   a. Poppy has 522 books. She puts the books on 3 bookshelves, sharing them equally. How many books are there on each bookshelf?

   b. A farmer is collecting apples. She puts 4 kilograms of apples in each basket. She fills 28 baskets and has 3 kilograms of apples left over. What mass of apples does she have altogether?

   c. There were 365 days in 2018. How many weeks is that? How many days are left over?

Level **B**

Write 3, 7, 8 and 9 in the boxes to give the greatest quotient.

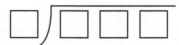

Write 3, 7, 8 and 9 in the boxes to give the smallest quotient.

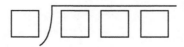

1. What is the greatest number that can be written in the space to make the calculation true?

$5 \times (\quad) < 42$ $\qquad$ $4 \times (\quad) < 33$ $\qquad$ $7 \times (\quad) < 24$

2. Estimate how many digits the quotient will have and calculate, using the column method.

$742 \div 7 =$
Estimate:
Quotient is a ( )-digit number

$907 \div 3 =$
Estimate:
Quotient is a ( )-digit number

$807 \div 8 =$
Estimate:
Quotient is a ( )-digit number

$850 \div 5 =$
Estimate:
Quotient is a ( )-digit number

3. Are the following calculations correct? Put a tick (✓) for 'correct' or a cross (✗) for 'incorrect' in the brackets. Then show the correct calculation for any that are wrong.

```
      2 3            3 0 6           2   4           1 0 2
   3) 6 9 0       2) 6 1 2        2) 4 0 9        4) 4 1 8
      6               6              4               4
     ___            _____          ___             _____
        9             1 2              9                 8
        9             1 2              8                 8
     ___            _____          ___             _____
        0               0              1                 0
      (   )           (   )          (   )           (   )
```

The correct calculation:

4. Read each question carefully and work out the answer.

   a. A coloured streamer is 525 centimetres long. How many lengths of 5 centimetres can be cut from the streamer?

   b. A swallow can eat 780 insects in 2 days. If it eats the same number every day, how many will it eat in one day?

   c. Each class in a year has the same number of books. Calculate how many books each class in each year has.

Year	Number of classes	Total number of books	The number of books in each class
Two	4	640	
Three	3	507	
Four	4	768	
Five	4	804	

Level **B**

1. Alex thinks of a number that, when multiplied by 6, will get a product in the range from 620 to 640.
This number may be (   ).

2. 48☐ ÷ 4 has 1 as a remainder, the number that could be written in the ☐ is (   ).

Pupil Textbook page 43

Level A

1. Estimate how many digits the quotient will have and calculate using the column method.

368 ÷ 4 =
Estimate: The quotient is a ( )-digit number

830 ÷ 4 =
Estimate: The quotient is a ( )-digit number

724 ÷ 9 =
Estimate: The quotient is a ( )-digit number

206 ÷ 3 =
Estimate: The quotient is a ( )-digit number

2. Use the column method to calculate and then check the answer.

385 ÷ 5 =

227 ÷ 3 =

3. Read each question carefully and work out the answer.

a. The road from Basingstoke to Rugby is 152 kilometres long. A car has been travelling for 2 hours. If it travels the same distance every hour, how far does it travel in 1 hour?

b. Carnations are sold in bunches of 8. How many bunches of carnations can be made up from 326 flowers? How many flowers are left?

c. Alice bought 7 rugby balls. Each ball cost £47 and she had £39 left. How much money did Alice take with her?

d. The school sports team bought 6 footballs for £276. What is the unit price of a football?

---

1. ☐ 20 ÷ 4, when ☐ is replaced with ( ), the quotient must have a 0 in the middle of the number; when ☐ is replaced with ( ), the quotient must have a 0 at the end of the number.

2. Think about this. In the following column calculation, the number in the tens place may be ( ).

$$7 \overline{\smash{)}\, 4\,\square\,\square}$$

4 Dividing by a one-digit number

Pupil Textbook page 44

1. Estimate how many digits the quotient will have and calculate, using the column method.

378 ÷ 4 =
Estimate: The quotient is a
(   )-digit number

378 ÷ 6 =
Estimate: The quotient is a
(   )-digit number

519 ÷ 7 =
Estimate: The quotient is a
(   )-digit number

426 ÷ 5 =
Estimate: The quotient is a
(   )-digit number

2. Look at the bar model and write the number sentence to calculate the answer.

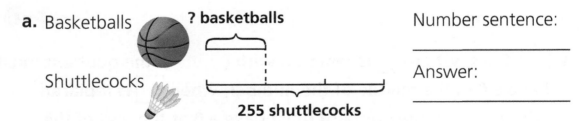

a. Basketballs   **? basketballs**

Shuttlecocks

255 shuttlecocks

Number sentence:
_____

Answer:
_____

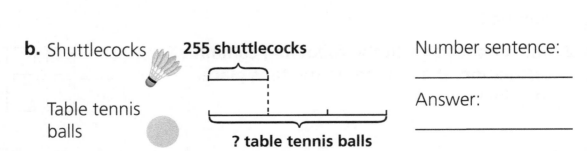

b. Shuttlecocks   **255 shuttlecocks**

Table tennis balls

? table tennis balls

Number sentence:
_____

Answer:
_____

58

3. Read each question carefully and work out the answer.

   a. A sea lion's mass is 378 kilograms, which is 9 times the mass of a penguin. What is the mass of the penguin?

   b. The Olympic torch relay team covered 612 kilometres in 3 days. How far was the torch carried each day, on average?

Level **B**

1. Think about this number sentence. To make the quotient have a 0 in the middle, (   ) can be written in the ☐.

$$3 \overline{)\ 9\ \boxed{}\ 4}$$

2. Complete the column calculation.

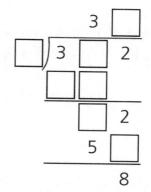

3. Dylan and Emma are picking apples. Dylan picks 152 apples in 2 hours. Emma picks 36 apples in half an hour. Who is faster?

59

4. Applications of division

Pupil Textbook page 45

Read each question carefully and work out the answer.

a. Dylan takes £100 to buy children's books. Each book costs £7, on average. What is the maximum number of books he can buy?
How much money will he have left?

b. Arthur is making fans. Each fan has 3 fan blades. How many fans can Arthur make if he has 61 fan blades?

c. There are 37 pupils in Emma's class. Every two pupils share a desk. How many desks does the class need?

d. My sister has bought a box of 114 flowers. She puts them into vases, with 5 flowers in each vase. What is the smallest number of vases she needs?

34 pupils go boating. Each big boat can take 6 people and the hire charge is £15. Each small boat can take 4 people and the hire charge is £12. How many of each boat should the teacher hire, to spend the minimum amount of money?

She should hire (   ) big boats and (   ) small boats.

5. Unit price, quantity and total price

Pupil Textbook pages 46–47

1. Fill in the missing information.

Item	Quantity	Unit price (£)	Total price (£)
notebook	6	4	
ball pen	3		15
pencil case		7	35

2. Read each question carefully and work out the answer.

a. Shilling Primary School bought 5 kettles. The unit price of a kettle is £36. Then the school bought 2 tea urns for £205 in all. How much did the school spend altogether?

b. Joe takes £200 to buy stationery for the school. He spends £120 on notebooks. He uses the rest of the money to buy 5 identical pens. How much does each pen cost?

c. Dylan wants to buy a tracksuit. The jacket is £60, the trousers are £40. How much would it cost to buy two tracksuits?

6. Practice exercise (3)

Pupil Textbook page 48

Level **A**

1. Write the answer.

$27 \div 9 =$

$270 \div 9 =$

$76 \div 2 =$

$112 \div 7 =$

$360 \div 9 + 4 =$

$29 - 92 \div 4 =$

2. Use the column method to complete these divisions. Write the checking process for the number sentence marked with *.

$641 \div 8 =$

$418 \div 9 =$

* $648 \div 6 =$

3. Fill in the missing numbers.

a. If the quotient of the number sentence 4 ☐ 9 ÷ 4 has 0 in the middle of the number, (   ) can be written in the ☐.

b. If the quotient of the number sentence 895 ÷ ☐ is a three-digit number, (   ) can be written in the ☐.

4. Read each question carefully and work out the answer.

a. There are two kinds of pen in a shop and their unit prices are £5 and £7 respectively. Mr Fisher spent £275 on one kind of pen. What kind of pen did Mr Fisher buy? How many?

b. A farmer picks fruit from peach, pear and apple trees. He picks 348 kilograms of peaches. The mass of the pears he picks is half the mass of the peaches. The mass of the peaches is half the mass of the apples he picks. How many kilograms of pears and apples does he have in total?

Dylan goes to buy stationery, but he has spilled something on his list.

Can you help him to calculate the unit price of a notebook?

Item	Unit price	Quantity	Total price
box of notebooks		6 boxes of notebooks	£183
box of pens	£75	1 box of pens	

Unit Five: Measure and geometry

What shapes can you see that have line symmetry?

The table below lists the sections in this unit.

After completing each section, assess your work.

(Use 😊 if you are satisfied with your progress or 😐 if you are not satisfied.)

Section	Self-assessment
1. Introduction to kilometres	
2. Metres and centimetres	
3. Symmetric shapes	
4. Classification of triangles (2)	
5. Area	
6. Areas of rectangles and squares	
7. Square metres	

1. Introduction to kilometres

Pupil Textbook pages 50–53

Level **A**

1. **Write the appropriate length unit ('metre' or 'kilometre') in the brackets.**

Ride about 300 (   ) per minute   Drive about 80 (   ) per hour

2. **Fill in the missing numbers.**

   a. 10 × 100 metres = (   ) metres. This can also be written as
   (   ) kilometre.

   b. The length of one lap of a stadium running track is 400 metres.
   When Ravi completes (   ) laps and then another (   )
   metres, he will have run a total of 1 kilometre.

   c. Alex takes 3 strides to walk 1 metre. If he walks for 1 kilometre,
   he needs to make (   ) strides.

3. **Convert these units.**

   3 km = (   ) m   20 km = (   ) m
   2000 m = (   ) km   50 000 m = (   ) km

4. **Write >, = or < in each ◯.**

   500 m ◯ 5 km   70 km ◯ 7000 m
   4 km + 800 m ◯ 4800 m   15 000 m − 5000 m ◯ 5 km

5. Read the question carefully and work out the answer.

The school, Charlie's home and Anya's home are all on the same road. Whose home is closer to the school? How far is it from Anya's home to Charlie's home?

Charlie's home   1 km   600 m   Anya's home

School

Quick practice

a. Some pupils stand in a line, hand in hand, as shown. How many pupils need to stand in the line to make it about 10 metres long?

b. How many pupils need to stand in a line, hand in hand, to make it a line 1000 metres long?

2. Metres and centimetres

Pupil Textbook page 54

Level **A**

1. First, estimate the length of this line, in centimetres.
Then measure the line, to see whether your estimate is correct.

(   ) centimetres

2. Write suitable units in the brackets.

Length of a skipping rope is 250 (   ).

Height of a flagpole is 15 (   ).

Length of an eraser is 4 (   ).

3. Write >, = or < in each ◯.

650 m ◯ 65 m   32 m ◯ 3200 cm   1 m 65 cm ◯ 1650 cm

4. Read each question carefully and work out the answer.

a. Ryan's height   Daisy's height

1 m 34 cm   1 m 40 cm

(   ) is taller than (   ).

b. The height of a sycamore tree   The height of a willow

3 m 75 cm   278 cm

(   ) is taller than (   ).

Level **B**

1. A rope is 10 metres long. How many centimetres are left after Laura cuts off 35 centimetres?

2. Write the lengths in the spaces, in the correct order.

2 m   20 cm   1 m 20 cm   2 m 10 cm

(   ) > (   ) > (   ) > (   )

3. Symmetric shapes

Pupil Textbook pages 55–56

Level **A**

1. Which of these shapes are symmetrical? Which are not symmetrical? If the shape is symmetrical, put a tick (✓) in the brackets. If it isn't symmetrical, put a cross (✗) in the brackets.

(   )   (   )   (   )

2. Draw the lines of symmetry on these shapes.

a.    b.    c.

3. Using the black thick line as the line of symmetry, draw the other half of each of the shapes below to make it a symmetric shape.

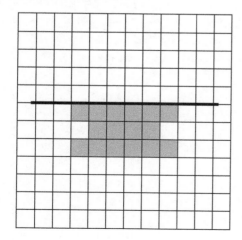   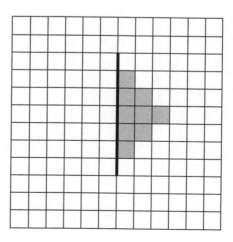

Quick practice

Can you draw a line of symmetry on these shapes?
What other shapes can you think of that are symmetrical?

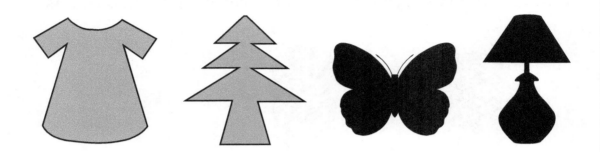

4. Classification of triangles (2)

Pupil Textbook pages 57–61

Level **A**

1. Look at the shapes below and read the descriptions in the question. Write the numbers of the shapes that match the properties described.

1.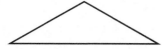
2.
3.

4.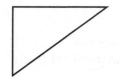
5.
6.

7.
8.
9.

a. Triangle: _____.

b. Right-angled triangle: _____, acute triangle: _____, obtuse triangle: _____.

c. Isosceles triangle: _____, equilateral triangle: _____.

2. Fill in the missing numbers and words.

a. A triangle is a shape enclosed by (   ) line segments, which has (   ) edges and (   ) angles.

b. If a triangle has exactly two equal edges, it is an (   ) triangle.

c. A triangle with three equal edges is called an (   ) triangle. It is also called a (   ) triangle, which has (   ) lines of symmetry.

71

3. True or false? Put a tick (✓) for 'true' or a cross (✗) for 'false' in the brackets.

   a. Every triangle is a symmetric shape. ( )

   b. All isosceles triangles are acute triangles. ( )

   c. In an equilateral triangle three sides are equal
   and three angles are equal. ( )

4. Draw the lines of symmetry on the two triangles below.

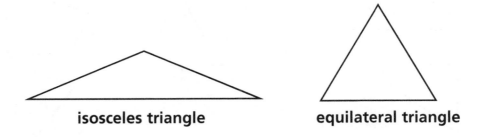

isosceles triangle   **equilateral triangle**

5. Fill in the missing numbers.

   a. Isosceles triangle

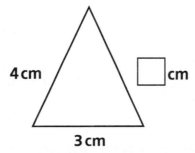

4 cm   ☐ cm

3 cm

   b. Equilateral triangle

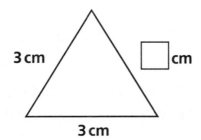

3 cm   ☐ cm

3 cm

c. In this diagram there are (   ) isosceles triangles.

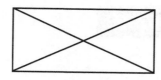

d. A triangle can be folded in three different ways, as shown in the diagram below. After folding, the three folded triangles can be placed exactly one over the other. This is an (   ) triangle with (   ) lines of symmetry.

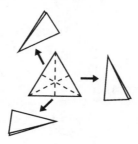

1. In this diagram there are (   ) triangles. There are (   ) isosceles triangles. (Measure to find out, and mark each pair of equal sides differently.)

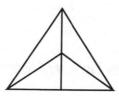

2. This diagram is composed of equilateral triangles of side 1 cm. There are (   ) equilateral triangles with sides of length 1 cm and (   ) equilateral triangles with sides of length 2 cm.

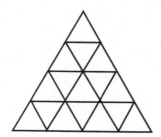

5. Area

Pupil Textbook pages 62–63

1. Draw and colour.

a. Colour the inside of the island green. Colour the pier red. Colour the beach yellow.

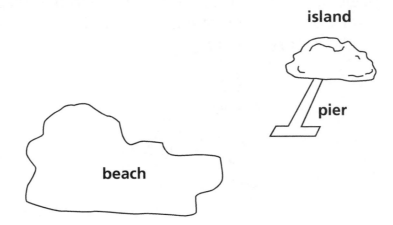

island

pier

beach

b. Compare the sizes of the beach, the island and the pier.

The area of the (   ) > the area of the (   ) > the area of the (   )

2. How large are the shapes below? Write the number of squares.

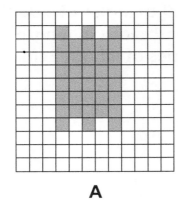

A

B

(   ) squares   (   ) squares

3. Which is larger, shape A or shape B?
(In both shapes, A and B, all the small squares are equal.)

A

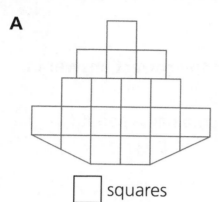

B

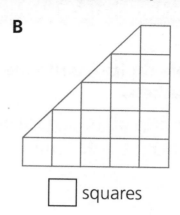

☐ squares

☐ squares

Comparison: The area of shape A ◯ the area of shape B.

Quick practice

Draw a shape that has an area of 10 squares.

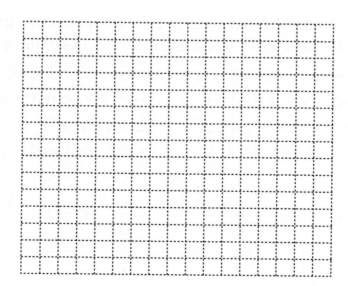

6. Areas of rectangles and squares

Pupil Textbook pages 64–65

1. **Multiple choice – write the letter of the correct answer in the brackets.**

    a. The area of the surface of your thumb nail is about (   ).
        A. $1\,cm^2$ **B.** $5\,cm^2$ **C.** $10\,cm^2$ **D.** $1\,cm$

    b. The area of the stamp in the picture
        on the right is (   ).
        A. $4\,cm^2$ **B.** $6\,cm^2$ **C.** $10\,cm^2$ **D.** $15\,cm^2$

2. **On the square grid below, each square represents one square centimetre. Draw the shape described and calculate its area.**

    a. A rectangle with length 4 centimetres, width 2 centimetres.
        The area of the rectangle is (   ) square centimetres.
    b. A square with a side length of 3 centimetres.
        The area of the square is (   ) square centimetres.

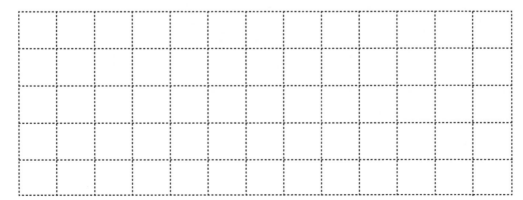

3. Measure each shape and calculate its area.

(   )cm

(   )cm

(   )cm

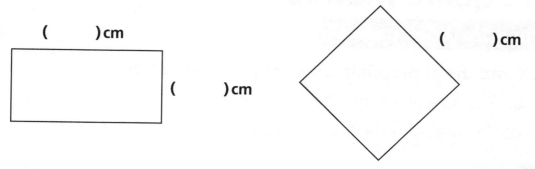

Draw a rectangle with an area of 12 square centimetres on this square grid. (Each square represents one square centimetre.)

How many different rectangles can you draw?

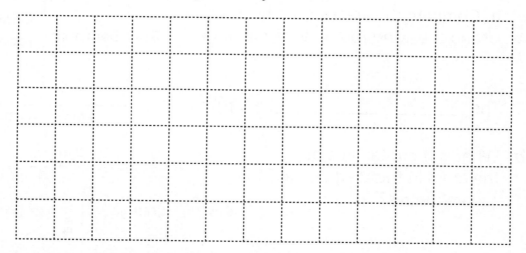

⭐ **Magic secrets**

The secret of Emma's magic puzzle (page 93). This picture shows the secret of Emma's magic. Look at the picture carefully and you will understand the secret behind her magic.

7. Square metres

Pupil Textbook page 66

Level **A**

1. Write the appropriate area units in the brackets.

    a. The area of a square table is about 1 (   ).

    b. The area of a classroom is about 40 (   ).

2. Read each question carefully and work out the answer.

    a. The following diagram is a plan of part of Alex's house. Calculate the areas, as described.

      i. What is the area of the living room?

      ii. Compare the areas of the bedroom and the living room,. Which is larger?

      The (_____) is larger.

1 m	balcony	
6 m	bedroom	living room
	4 m	3 m

    b. What is the total area of the grass in this diagram, in square metres?

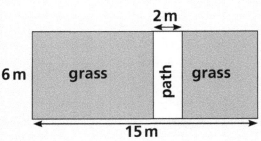

2 m

6 m   grass   path   grass

15 m

    c. The area of a playground is 261 square metres. The width of the playground is 9 metres. What is the length, in metres?

Level **B**

This is a rectangular field. Its length is 8 metres and its width is 5 metres. A square paddock is fenced off, of the maximum possible size. What area of the original field is left over, in square metres?

5 m

8 m

Unit Six: Consolidating and enhancing

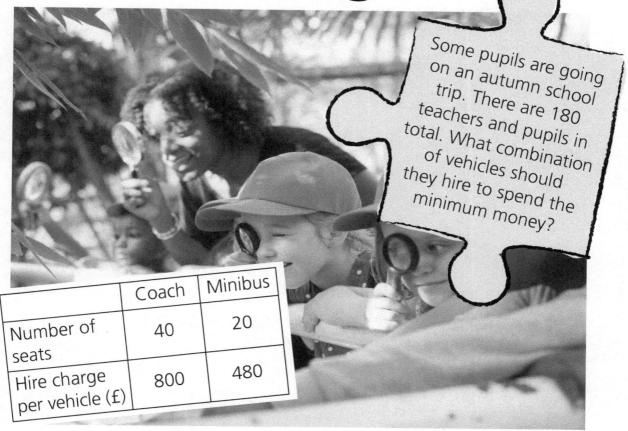

Some pupils are going on an autumn school trip. There are 180 teachers and pupils in total. What combination of vehicles should they hire to spend the minimum money?

	Coach	Minibus
Number of seats	40	20
Hire charge per vehicle (£)	800	480

The table below lists the sections in this unit.

After completing each section, assess your work.

(Use 😊 if you are satisfied with your progress or 😕 if you are not satisfied.)

Section	Self-assessment
1. Multiplication and division	
2. Problem solving	
3. Building shapes	
4. How large are they?	
5. Calculating the areas of rooms	

1. Multiplication and division

Level **A**

1. **Use the column method to calculate. Check your answers to the questions marked with *.**

$29 \times 8 =$

$241 \div 4 =$

$304 \times 9 =$

$903 \div 9 =$

$7 \times 830 =$

$*617 \div 5 =$

2. Complete the row calculations.

$804 \div 4 + 201$

$5960 - 960 \div 2$

$607 \times 8 - 856$

$24 + 76 \times 6$

3. Read each question carefully and work out the answer.

  a. The school bought 4 sets of fans. How much did they cost in total?

£280 per set

b. A farmer has 8 and 448 .

How many times greater is the number of goats than the number of sheep?

c. Jacob learned 196 spellings in a week. How many did he learn every day, on average?

d. A shop sold 18 boxes of apples, each holding 8 kg, and had 128 kg left over. How many kilograms of apples were there in the shop at first?

Write the missing numbers in the boxes.

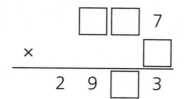

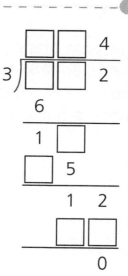

Pupil Textbook pages 70–71

1. Work out how to get the numbers in the second row from the numbers in the first row, then fill in the missing numbers.

3	8	11	84	120	351	809
15	40	55				

2. Write >, = or < in each ◯ to make the number sentence true.

$27 \div 3$ ◯ $72 \div 3$　　　$160 \div 2$ ◯ $106 \div 2$　　$315 \div 7$ ◯ $315 \div 9$

$72 \div 9$ ◯ $64 \div 8$　　　$630 \div 3$ ◯ $990 \div 9$　　$567 \div 7$ ◯ $656 \div 8$

3. Read each question carefully and work out the answer.

　a. A car travelled 360 kilometres in 4 hours. How many kilometres did this car travel per hour?

　b. The same brand of pet food is sold in large and small packs in the supermarket. The price of the small pack, with 3 cans, is £12. The price of the large pack, with 5 cans, is £15. Compare the prices to find out which pack offers the lower price per can.

2. Problem solving

Pupil Textbook pages 72–74

Level **A**

1. Look at each line segment diagram. Complete the calculations, showing all your steps.

a.

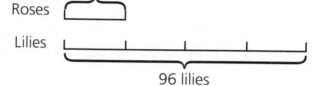

How many roses?

Roses

Lilies

96 lilies

b.

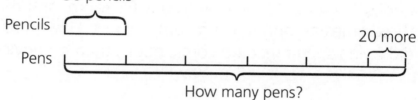

36 pencils

Pencils

20 more

Pens

How many pens?

c.

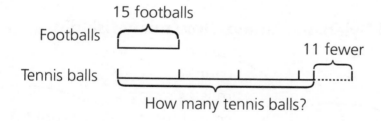

15 footballs

Footballs

11 fewer

Tennis balls

How many tennis balls?

d.

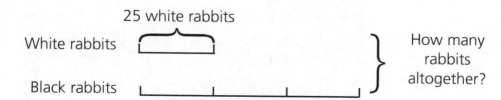

25 white rabbits

White rabbits

Black rabbits

How many rabbits altogether?

2. Read each question carefully and work out the answer.

    a. Some gardeners were planting willows and pine trees along a roadside. They planted 56 pine trees. The number of willows was 30 less than 4 times the number of pine trees. How many willows did they plant?

    b. One chair costs £12 and the price of the table is five times that of the chair. How much money do I need to buy a table and a chair?

    c. On Saturday morning, Dylan tidied his room and read comic books. He took 20 minutes to tidy his room, and then spent three times as long reading comic books. How much more time did Dylan spend reading comic books than on tidying his room?

Level **B**

Emma, Alex and Dylan are fishing. How many fish did Dylan catch?

I caught 2 times as many fish as Emma.

I caught 8 fish.

I caught 3 more than 2 times as many as Alex.

1. Complete these calculations, showing all the steps in your working.

$52 \times 9 \times 4$

$488 \times 6 \div 8$

$336 \div 8 \div 3$

2. Read each question carefully and work out the answer.

   a. How much does each pen cost?

There are 8 pens in each box and the total cost is £160.

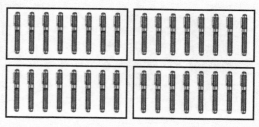

   b. How many kilograms of apples does each person pick?

4 workers picked 6 baskets of apples altogether, and each basket had a mass of 38 kg.

3. How many pots of flowers did the school buy to decorate the classrooms?

The school building has 3 floors, and there are 5 classrooms on each floor.

We put 4 pots of flowers in each classroom.

4. Cashmere jumpers cost £140 each.

£140

It costs the same to buy 7 cashmere jumpers as it does to buy 5 coats. How much does one coat cost?

5. The toy factory made 180 toys. 4 toys were packed into each small box. Then 5 small boxes were packed into each large box. How many large boxes were filled?

6. In a supermarket, there are 20 boxes of bananas. There are twice as many boxes of oranges as boxes of bananas, and there are 3 times as many boxes of apples as boxes of oranges. How many boxes of apples are there?

1. **Intelligent practice – think about the best way to do each calculation.**

   $125 \times 9 \times 8$

   $25 \times (59 + 59 + 59 + 59)$

2. **Some pupils are going on an autumn school trip. The total number of teachers and pupils is 180. A coach has 40 seats and costs £800 to hire. A minibus has 20 seats and costs £480 to hire.**

   The school should hire (   ) coaches and (   ) minibuses so that the total cost is as low as possible, and the cost will be £(   ).

3. Building shapes

1. Write the names of the shapes.

_____ _____ _____
_____ _____ _____

_____ _____
_____ _____

2. Write the numbers of the triangles in the correct spaces. Measure the sides if you need to.

1. 2. 3. 4.

5. 6. 7. 8.

Acute triangle: _____ Isosceles triangle: _____

Right-angled triangle: _____ Equilateral triangle: _____

Obtuse triangle: _____

3. Count the shapes and fill in the missing numbers.

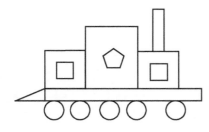

There are (   ) △
There are (   ) ▭
There are (   ) ⬠
There are (   ) □
There are (   ) ○

1. Practice

a. Draw a straight line to cut an angle from a hexagon. How many angles does the new shape have? (Trace the picture and cut it out. Try as many ways as you can.)

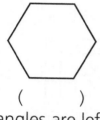      

(   ) angles are left   (   ) angles are left   (   ) angles are left

b. Design a floor tile of your own and draw it on the square grid below.

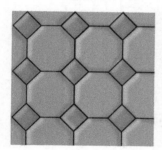

2. Read the question carefully and work out the answer.

How many bricks are needed to fill the hole in the wall? Count bricks to find out.

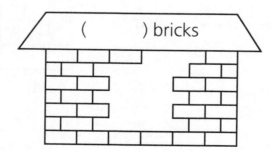

(   ) bricks

4. How large are they?

Pupil Textbook page 80

1. How many squares does each shaded shape cover? Each square represents 1 cm². What is the area, in square centimetres?

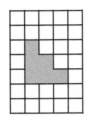

Covers (   ) squares
The area is (   ) cm².

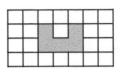

Covers (   ) squares
The area is (   ) cm².

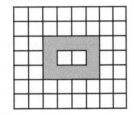

Covers (   ) squares
The area is (   ) cm².

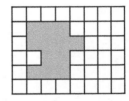

Covers (   ) squares
The area is (   ) cm².

2. Each small square in the diagram represents 1 cm².

The area of shape 1 is (   ) cm².

The area of shape 2 is (   ) cm².

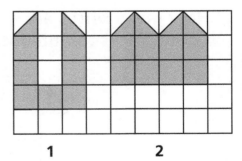

1   2

What is the area of each of the shapes below?
(Each small square represents 1 cm².)

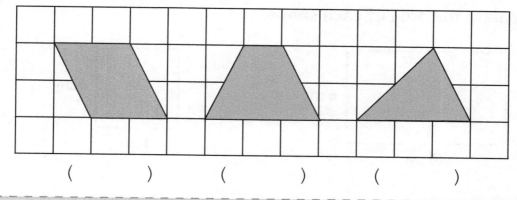

(   )   (   )   (   )

✦ Mathematical magic

Magic tangrams

Tangrams were invented in China and have spread widely across the world.

The tangram is an amazing educational toy with endless variations.

Emma and Poppy were playing with their tangrams at the weekend.

Emma said mysteriously to Poppy: 'Poppy, did you know, I can use a tangram to do tricks? Look at these two pictures, they are built up from the same tangram pieces. There are two different figures in the picture. Their upper bodies are almost the same, but one has feet and one has no feet. However, they really are both built from the same tangram shapes!'

Poppy was very puzzled about this. Can you think why? What is the secret of this magic?

Can you help Poppy to solve the mystery?

Try out some tangram magic with your classmates or family.

Find the secret behind Emma's magic somewhere in this book.

5. Calculating the areas of rooms

Pupil Textbook page 81

1. Calculate the area of each shape.

6 cm

10 cm

4 cm

4 cm

2. Read this question carefully and work out the answer.

Here is a plan of Laura's house. All the lengths are in metres. Calculate the total area of her house. Give your answer in square metres.

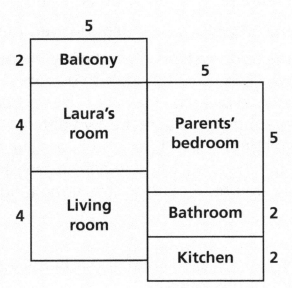

5

2 | Balcony

5

4 | Laura's room

Parents' bedroom | 5

4 | Living room

Bathroom | 2

Kitchen | 2

1. Calculate the area of this shape. All the lengths are in centimetres.

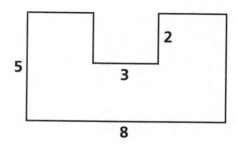

2. This shape is made up of 4 identical smaller rectangles. The shorter side of a small rectangle is known to be 2 centimetres long. Calculate the area of the large rectangle.

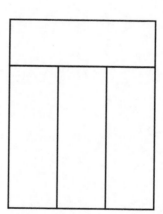